LOOK AT IT THIS WAY

LOOK AT IT THIS WAY

Derek Coggrave

Poems © Derek Coggrave, 2024

Cover images: 'Schrodinger's Cat Alive' (front jacket) &
'Schrodinger's Cat Dead' (back jacket) © Derek Coggrave

All rights reserved

ISBN: 978-1-9164789-3-0

ACKNOWLEDGEMENTS

Thanks to the editors of *The Friday Poem* and 'Poetry Corner' in *Barnet Borough Times*, where two of these poems were previously published.

Design & typesetting: Nell Nelson

First published in 2024
by Stravaigers Press
21 Hatton Green, Glenrothes KY7 4SD

The right of Derek Coggrave to be identified
as author of this work has been asserted in accordance
with the Copyright, Designs & Patent Act, 1988

Printed and bound by Imprint Digital, Exeter
https://digital.imprint.co.uk

Contents

I: Situation Report

  The Green Man / 11
  Bonnie's Mouse / 12
  Nighy / 13
  Hat / 14
  The Unsuccessful Declutterer / 15
  Karen / 16
  Downsizing / 17
  Situation Report / 18

II: The Writing Business

  Bookcase / 21
  Covering Letter to Poetry Editor / 22
  Nothingness / 24
  How to Keep the Poetry Dracula Buried / 26
  In Support of Bad Writing / 28
  Postscript to Poetry Editor / 30

III: Memories

  i / 33
  ii / 34
  iii / 35
  iv / 36
  v / 37
  vi / 38
  vii / 40

IV: Look At It This Way

  Look at it this way / 42
  Answers on a Postcard Please / 46
  Birdbrains / 47
  Builders / 48
  'Is This the Answer to Everything: 42?' / 49
  Our Forbidden Planet: The Id / 50
  Russian Roulette / 52

V: *Mortality*

Perfect Body or Perfect Mind? / 55
Humanity's Beating Heart / 56
Sand / 58
The Crow / 59
An Alzheimer's Test for Nonagenarians / 60
3 December, 2023 / 61
The Fly / 62
Jack and Jill / 63
X-Rays and Dreaming of Tattoos / 64

VI: *Time and Tide*

Lions / 67
Match Point / 68
Regrets / 69
Letter from an Island in the Sun / 70
The Usual / 72
Time / 73
The Time Machine / 74
You Have Been Selected / 76
Tree / 78
Tom / 79

Notes on the poems / 83

In memory of
Hew Koh

Foreword

I have been asked, 'What is the incentive for writing poetry?' For many human activities, the incentive is financial. Write a best seller and it can make millions. However, writing such books does require a talent for characterisation, imaginative plots and skilful writing. Success is not easily achieved.

Communicating in writing has, nevertheless, been critical for the development of our social constructs over millennia. The control we exert over our economic development would have been impossible without it. Thus, the desire to write something is an essential part of our genome, although this may decrease as writing becomes less important in the process of gaining an education (thanks to AI and other tools).

Another key factor may be that some of us like to indulge in particular interests. After all, the proportion of golfers with a zero handicap is small. But that doesn't stop others from using their weekends in the mostly hopeless task of trying to reach such heights. In the same way, we poetasters will not all become internationally recognised poets. However, those such as myself keep indulging, largely because we find it an interesting, enjoyable and sometimes irresistible pastime. There's also the hope that with enough practice our handicap might improve.

Finally, as I mention in 'Perfect Body or Perfect Mind?' (p. 55), writing poetry will help to keep our our minds intact, especially as we grow older — so much better than staring at screens.

If you do indulge in writing poetry, however, do not give up the day job. You need to eat.

D.C.

I
SITUATION REPORT

THE GREEN MAN

You see how they prattle on about their age
as if it's worth a jot? Him
one hundred years odd, her even more.
Vacant thoughts. Zimmer frames. A limp.
Trembling hands. Assorted sticks. They move
like tumbleweed tilting in the breeze.
Wheelchairs as backup in the airport, museum,
parking lot. But what's the point of carrying on
when doing anything's beyond them?

I'm different. A mutated gene has left me
living after more than a thousand years.
You've found pals in *The Green Man*, beer
drinkers just like you. You walk beneath
my mugshot every time you're here. I was
viewed with awe till I passed 130. Then
the chaos of war. Abandoned in the woods.
Forgotten. Left to drift alone, the link lost.
I roamed, growing calluses, picking up
lichen, caked with fungi, hair full of galls.
Blood still flowed in my veins but slowly,
slowly, changed into sap. Roots took hold.
Time rolled past. Now green from head to foot,
I might be anywhere you look.

BONNIE'S MOUSE

That first time she dropped the mouse
on the grass by my feet, and tapped
the fear-frozen body with her paw
like a child nudging a wind-up toy,
Then, distracted, she let it slip away.

The second time it was pouched
inside her cheeks, the tail dribbling
down her jaw, her bite too hard.
We watched it try to escape,
haul its body along by its front legs,
the back legs limp as stale lettuce.
Burning the mind, the pain. I raised
the shovel. *What are you doing?*
said Hew Koh. *Taking the agony away*,
I said. *No!* she cried. *Look at its tiny eyes.
It's watching us.* I tumbled it back
into the compost heap.
                        Awake
that night I thought of the mouse.
How could God (if God exists) go on,
aware of each miserable event?

The third time, I took the mouse
and slipped it back into the compost heap.
Its back legs were running. *I know
it's the same one. See? Still lame.*

Now every day I put mouse-sized
loaves of bread under a nearby
dustbin lid and wonder if the mouse
believes in miracles …

NIGHY

Feral, black, flashing white canines, he slipped in
through the cat-flap, ate Meow Meow's food,
pissed my washing machine brown.

I bought a chip-reader, shut the flap,
moved to scoop him up. In three seconds
he ripped the flap frame from the door and fled.

Cat-burglar, escape artist, he would have been
in and out of Colditz as if access was
by revolving door. I laid a trap.

Neutered by the RSPCA, he moved in,
grew fat, then constipated, stopped eating,
began to fade away. I tried *Lax-A-Past*

and now he's back. When I put his food bowl down
he rubs his cheek against my hand. Bats it away
(claws retracted) if I try to stroke his back.

When a strange face appears, he's off.
In cat years, he's a nonagenarian. If I'm lucky
I'll live longer by a whisker. Keep him safe.

He digs holes almost as deep as me.
In all the wrong places.

HAT

When she died
Hew Koh's floppy blue sun-hat
capped the stout oak-post
where she had left it
at the bottom of the stairs.
Handy for cooking, she always said,
to keep the smell of food
from mingling with her hair.

The mix of her and her cooking lingered,
gradually faded. The hat grew dusty
and was washed and returned
to where I can make touch
— *good morning!* —
as I reach the bottom stair.
And, when the phone rings,
I let her know who made the call,
give a fair wind of what we said.

I like to think her spirit's still around
although I can't be sure that this is fair.
But it's my best attempt to make it seem
as if she's there.

THE UNSUCCESSFUL DECLUTTERER

The stumps, bat & ball I used four decades ago
(cricket with my nephew by the brook).
My grandfather's chisels & files. My father's plane.
The letters & postcards that you collected
for fifty years, a biography of our friends.
Our wedding album (smiling aunts & uncles,
friends). Photo: me sitting on my grandfather's
knee, his prickly moustache. In the back room,
the chest of drawers he made. Copies of
thousands of my letters written to sundry
recipients, stacked chronologically.
Poems/emails filed. On surfaces & the floor,
scattered newspapers, typed drafts. Twenty
trolley-loads of books & other stuff to Oxfam
(I did try). Schoolboy algebra, Kinglake's *Eothen*.
The echoes of your footsteps & your voice.
In the bedroom cupboard, your ashes
to scatter with mine at a forest edge, in time.

KAREN

In memoriam

The landscape of our lives forms slowly as we age
and the distant lands, for which I once craved,
lose their urgency. My cat and I prefer close, not far away.
A walk in the local park, the familiar trees, the slides
where children play. Our local high street, a smile,
a familiar face, a short passing of the time of day.

I met Karen once when out and she listened
to stories of my cats. Meow Meow, her long
white fur with a touch of ginger, grey, known to charm
even the toughest frame of mind. I wrote a short history
of how Meow Meow gradually moved in with us
when her owner left. Then Nighy, the feral cat

adopted me, and Meow Meow agreed that both
he and I could remain. Following our chat
I dropped the note, our history, into the surgery
and a photo of MM, which Karen placed on view
for those who waited in reception to make a date.
When my late wife phoned the surgery, she always

wished that Karen would take the call. Cheerful,
caring, a friendly greeting and a smile when
I was there. So sad to learn that Karen is no longer
of this world. Hence, the salient points: the topology
of our lives does change as time moves on
and the familiar landmarks of our home ground fade.

We live in a strange world: black holes, white holes,
wormholes, dark matter, dark energy, held in space
by gravity, contained by the speed of light. Thus,
if our universe is infinite, then inevitably our lives
will repeat and we'll make the same mistakes again.
A reason to be kind to those we meet, as Karen was.

DOWNSIZING

It stalks us, age. I glance back nervously
as each day trickles past, searching
the shadows for the silhouette of the ghost
that bears my name. Since Lockdown, I stay local.
The world I occupy is shrinking.
When last I entered the front door, it was
just wide enough for me to squeeze through.

All those tasks undone pile up. Journals,
books I have yet to read — stacked.
Sheets of virgin paper, tubes of paint,
the butt ends of charcoal, the colours
and bold strokes that I intend — a landscape,
a portrait, a life-form perfectly shaped
that has evolved to take root within my
consciousness. My camera dusty, unused.

A dresser drawer splintered, inclined,
is filled with sketches, dog-eared scraps
of poems (incomplete), from which
a cacophany of voices, alarmed by
my neglect, shriek, *Me, Me, Me.*
The walls are shrinking. Cracks widen.
The pictures I painted and hung there
shift awry, tilting, jostling for space.

The bookshelves skew, books fall —
an avalanche. The ceiling's lower.
The light swings closer to the floor.
I'm writing this letter quickly, just in case.
If I can't get out, I'll float it into the street
from an upstairs window, stamped first class.
Perhaps some kind soul will pick it up
        and pop it in the post.

SITUATION REPORT

The statistics show that those approaching ninety (me) who catch the Covid 19 virus have a 20% probability of death.

Now that you've gone, I'm alone. Saturday night,
no fever — yet. I'm watching *Passengers*.
Chris Pratt and Jennifer Lawrence together
on a star ship hurtling through space
(half light-speed) ninety years from being safe.

My situation isn't much different. Earth rotating
1041 mph, orbiting sun 70,000 mph, spinning
with galaxy 514,000 mph, my timeline grooved
into the universe at 495,000 mph (plus unknowns
for time of day). All this leaving me apparently
stationary. Still in space.

Although Jennifer Lawrence isn't here, I do
have *cat*. I'm missing a hologram and some kind
of robot-android thingy of the well-spoken,
argumentative sort. But for that, Saturday nights
in Finchley would be much like *Red Dwarf*.

Stardom? I'd give it all of it up
just to have you back.

II

THE WRITING BUSINESS

BOOKCASE

Gravity strengthens where poetry collects on shelves:
the plastic track holding the glass doors has sagged
leaving the doors propped against the wall.

Resurrection. I screw in place a solid beam of wood. But
when I invert the bookcase, the bottom track falls out
scattering twenty-seven matchsticks.

Twenty-seven matchsticks secreted by the previous
assembler. A bodge to cover up a poor design?
The cubed root of twenty-seven is three —

is this a message from a mathematician
or merely an indication that the assembler
had well-smoked lungs? I put the books back

on the shelves. I feel the tug of gravity increase,
begin to drag me down. This force of nature
might suck me in, leaving me rendered down

to one quixotic line of verse.

COVERING LETTER TO POETRY EDITOR

I am always reluctant to ask anyone to read
anything I write, in case they conclude
it was a waste of their time. And time is
the one essential tool that enables our lives.

I probably do not fit the normal profile
of those who submit. I'm a nonagenarian.
And technology has delivered social media,
texts, mobile phones and the metaverse,

which (as in the 'real' inflationary universe)
act like dark matter and dark energy,
driving the generations to drift further apart
within their social space. The real artist,

I infer, is nature. We are only here as observers,
anthropic. And what we paint or write —
the music we compose — is not essential. Thus,
our brief appearance, our self-importance,

can be assessed when our tenure on this earth
is measured against the time the universe
has been extant — even against what came before.
But we should learn everything we can

in the time allotted to us. Hence, the poems enclosed.
The probability of your deciding that these are
worthy to appear in print will have odds similar
to my successfully utilising the time spent waiting

for your answer ... to devise a theory
that will unite Einstein's General Theory of Relativity
with the hidden world that is quantized.
(I have assumed time is quantum in 'Memories VII'.)

NOTHINGNESS

The writing of this note was overseen
by a well-known cartoonist

A poem will be printed on the last page
of my new book. The typeface used will be
Shrinking Riscatype Pantin Lingt, 113.
This type was not sold commercially
because of its hazardous nature. Once
printed on the page, and each time the text

is viewed, it shrinks at an increasing rate
quickly approaching infinity. Potentially
such an experiment will test whether
a state of nothingness is possible
as in theory, the quantum objects that form
the words will shrink to a point where

all quantum structures implode, although
we do not think a state of nothingness
can be observed. Thus, after a risk assessment,
and taking into account all possible hazards,
Health and Safety have insisted a warning
must be placed on every page informing

the reader that the final page might trigger
a vanishing point where all matter, followed
by the reader and finally the book, might
be sucked into a self-destructing vacuum.
However, as stated, nothingness would obviate
an observer. This is not the primary problem.

The primary problem arises because if
the current structures that we experience
developed from nothingness, it suggests
all of this could be repeated *ad infinitum.*
Health and Safety insisted on this warning
as they believe the risk is not worth taking

if you see what I mean?

(This is not a poem.)

HOW TO KEEP THE POETRY DRACULA BURIED

After reading 'Down With Poetry' by Nell erm, what's-her-name

My prose (I can use it in a form that bores)
cures your insomnia — not completely
but just enough so that you can get hooked
and for a monthly stipend can always get
some more. I never 'found a voice' but I can

keep sending you my poetry.
This is a threat. You might end up finding
your PC is brain-dead and the contents
of your disk have been moved offshore.
My suggestion is to open an account

using a crypto-currency platform,
not to test your exposition and the quality
of 'voice' but to dissolve the brain clot
inside your PC, so that it can comprehend
the expletives you discharge as you obey.

Being, like my father, of an engineering bent,
when I read 'Parnassus', I had to look up
where he came from and where he went.
The word 'like'? Like' is a word, like with jaws —
like I always avoid, like. And as for that

subject, the Vernacular, it is a topic that
my cat dislikes or — to tell the truth — abhors.
Poetry (its many forms) is a forum for
reading on the train. It's not like
a newspaper and will never happen
that someone is hunched over you, stealing
your words, while you fear to turn the page.

This is written with the objective of
my remaining insignificant within
the poetry debate, at the same time as
ensuring that my nose remains unscathed.

This is too long to be added as a postscript on my grave.

IN SUPPORT OF BAD WRITING

I once heard, 'Only poor writers
use the word *so*'. My use of this word
dates back to poetry classes
with Michael Donaghy circa 1998.

He recommended reading Ted Hughes
and I bought his *Selected Poems*, part
Crow and *Birthday Letters*. Now
Michael Donaghy is tragically —

unexpectedly — dead, as is Ted Hughes,
and also my wife. All have vanished from
this wild ledge we occupy, that might
at any moment crumble beneath our feet,

send us tumbling into a dark abyss,
the unknown. If we could be aware
of the future — how terrifying!
I took the hint and wrote 'The Crow',

a hooded black shape stripping the carcass
of a rat. Life is tenuous. Gradually
those we have met will leave. No longer
can we recapitulate the past, exchange

news of old friends, the memories,
the backbone of shared lives. Ted Hughes' poem
'18 Rugby Street' began with the word 'So'.
I vaguely remember a discussion

between one who vehemently
defended its use, and someone else —
I've forgotten now. But thus,
I use the word *So* in memoriam.

POST SCRIPT TO POETRY EDITOR

If you reject my submission
the shredder can be put to good use,
although I hope without
an exaggerated display of exuberance.

III

MEMORIES

-i-

A nightmare repeated from before I could sense the past.
Unrelenting pressure around the ears. Breathless,
sightless, no sound, limbs paralysed. The end
of gestation perhaps? Trapped in the birth canal?

-ii-

My arm is caught in a vice-like grip. I'm shoved
into my bedroom. I stumble. The door bangs shut.
The key turns in the lock. I feel the chill of isolation.
Only imagination allows me to presume my tears
stopped. There were no repeats of this self-defining act.

-iii-

Sixpence from Woolworths, a scabbard holding a shiny sword.
Once home, I buckled them round my waist, raised
the sword with two hands above my head, and charged
into the garden to slay the dragon whose fiery taunts
coursed through my brain. Glory, and a damsel in distress —
these were in the script. But not the instruction *Trip*.
Short trousers meant both knees were stripped. The blood!

-iv-

English Lesson

It was a ritual, soon after my first day
in school. I remember the classroom,
the desks, monogrammed, iron-framed,
ink-stained, the slopped inkwells,
the groove for pens. The bare walls
(they may still echo our spelling mistakes).
I watched as my school friends
were called one by one to stand
at the teacher's side. Grey-haired,
a stoop, grumpy-stern. A face
worn by years of teaching
hated words. The girls were pinched
on the arm. The boys? Short trousers,
bare legs. Hesitate too long on a word
and the wooden ruler she kept at hand
would flash, the flat side on bare flesh.
I closed my eyes, waiting.
Heard the thwack.

-v-

Have you watched Film4? That intro, the images
of a deserted petrol station forecourt, each frame
sliding slowly up the screen, accelerating to a blur?
A burning tyre trundles into view. And as one
begins to form one's own theories as to why,
annoyingly the film begins to roll.

Looking back in time, a tough day, working late,
followed by the isolation of a long drive home.
There is a numbness induced by the pressure
to complete the scheduled tasks, while those who
were the incentive for my efforts to provide
and to survive have left for a foreign land ...

This leaves a question posed by the road ahead.
An endless row of identical lamp-posts flickers by
Did this iteration of the same event occur
to make a point? Should I go back
and — to each one — fix a note on which
I would etch the words:
                    'The End of Time'?

-vi-

The *Silindoeng*? I remember her like an old friend.
Sailing from Mombasa into a storm, her
three thousand tons rolled like a fairground ride.
When she was fully laden, one could dip
one's hand in the sea from her main deck.
Mombasa, then Madagascar, calling at Tananarive,
followed by Ile Sainte Marie. A handful of passengers,
we held a picnic on the latter's sandy beach.
The Dutch crew nicknamed her *The Submarine*.

Later, low on the horizon, the Maldives: the only land
we passed for weeks, no other ships in sight.
The steady vibration from the deck provided
a threadbare canvas for nature's brushstrokes.
Light splashed as a form of absolution, banishing
turmoil, restoring tranquillity to the conscious mind.
Fleetingly, flying fish crested the waves,
a gull gliding across our wake, and at night,
in the spindrift, fluorescence glowed,
hinting at mysteries in the deep ocean.

Listen to whispers of the bow-created waves.
A moment's awareness, caught within
a quantum glitch? This now separates
the uncertainties of the future from
the slow fragmentation of past events.
Thus slowed, time will form pools
in the shallows of the mind — still leave time
to hollow out a mould, in which to cast a mark
that asks the question why. Thoughts drift by.

See the sunset as nature's shifting colours lie
strewn across an ininterrupted arc of sky.
Watch the stars take hold in the slowly fading light.
Then you might search for the unknowns
that lie beyond our reach. After seventy years
have passed, how many of those who shared
those moments on that ship are ghosts?
                How many still survive?

The *Silindoeng* was built in 1949 and we met
some time in '53. After five weeks at sea,
we parted, I believe, the best of friends. I would
hope that she, the Silindoeng, could seek
solace in the presence of the *Marie Celeste*,
with whom to share the secrets of a last voyage —
for there is no record
            of her END.
                May she rest in peace.

-vii-

I prefer the Virgin Atlantic ad, the girl with her
hair tied back. Her eyes, open wide, turn quickly
to the camera as she steps onto the moving track.
Then the view is switched while her slender form
accelerates towards her destined vanishing point.
She trips crazily as she steps to firmer ground
and glances back momentarily over one shoulder,
revealing in that moment every facet of her
                            existential mind.

If Einstein's block universe cannot be claimed
as an answer for time's direction and for our
presence here, can this mean we will be preserved
as if in a giant block of amber, through which
each pixellated image, each fraction of a heartbeat
that counts down our days will be saved?
Will they be retained forever, these memories,
ready to be re-run in some future age? When I stumble,
glance back, will an observer wonder why
the acrid smoke, the white hot flames?

IV

LOOK AT IT THIS WAY

LOOK AT IT THIS WAY —

now that you are dead,
now that you have accepted my invitation,
we can begin with a question.
Do not hesitate, ask *What is it?*
Have you thought of what comes next,
that between now and then a great gulf is fixed?

No! You didn't think! You'd always thought
that later there would be time, time to prepare,
time to plan this last, this final visit.
But death came sooner than you had
                            any reason to expect.
Who are you? Where are you? In which one?

You have listened to the story of the multiverse?
No! Those who come here always prattle on
about promises not kept, their doubt, their indecision,
while the questions they would have had answered drift
as they talk of time passed in pub saloons,
of pool rooms veiled in drifting smoke,
of time spent on crowded, beer-stained floors
looking for the invitation of a lifted skirt,
of time spent in prayer, of spirits they could not invoke.
Time pauses, like vapour over clinking coffee cups.
Time ends, but still each overwhelming question floats.

As the European markets recovered from their early lows,
the August future's premium to cash rose.

At creation, one universe was planned
but through an oversight ...
Not God! Good heavens no!
Once started, it became an endless chain,
an infinity of universes, and still they bud.

And so we might ask you to participate.
Will you be like God? Hmm ... Some form
                of immortality, perhaps?
You must know that we will first examine
                every step you made.

Skim your tessera across the ripples of the burning lake.
Walk down each avenue you did not take.
Look in through the windows of each strange house.
Sift through the litter piled inside each door.
                Search for your name.
Look with care beyond each staircase you ascend.

You'll find against the sky the room you kept,
across whose vacant walls your mind
would trace the entangled lives of those
who came to your domain. Time to create,
time to instruct the actors who would
                bring you fame.
You lacking authenticity, the walls stared back,
leaving you unfinished, incomplete. The 'Get Lost'
motif on your vest, the jibe of a pointed finger,
your ripped jeans, signs of an overwhelming
lethargy measured by heaped beer cans
                accumulating at your feet
and leaving only one finished, sordid work of art:
the stained sheets of your grimy unmade bed.

Look at your shaved head, the tattos that swirl
up from calves, loins and chest
to grip your neck and which you vouch
were not intended as an image to offend.
Observe the wasteland you created from

the trash that you left trailing in your wake.
Look at your hand upon each door handle
                you open to pass through.
Watch your feet tread down each endless corridor.

The faces you once knew now glance back
from cracked mirrors, the moulds that stain
fissured plaster, from doors unhinged
and in whose peeling paint you see pareidolia,
the ghosts emerging from your past.
Watch the room dissolve as those
protecting walls that were projected from
another's mind fade slowly from your view.
Assemble such words on which you base your act.
Remember: all that you will see and think
lacks any certainty of being real, of being fact.

You arrived, you felt the Footman take your coat.
You saw all this while looking in the mirror.
He smirked: you were afraid.
Could you not recognise your face, your mirror image?
Some who come will say their animus was
                      'a perfect detonator'.
Others will say they wished that time was quicker,
waiting each day for that fifteen minutes
when the prophet claimed their fame would flicker.

They'll tell of time they spent accumulating pelf,
time which chipped away to form the profile
                of authentic self.

Remember the runtime of your youth? The facts
which came your way so you might grapple
with the mysteries of your brief stay?
Unsolicited perhaps, but you digressed, unread,
unable to float above the challenge of your

incipient kind. You chose instead seedy offbeat
basement clubs, the lure of a husky voice,
the lingering glance as those slim, pale hands
caressed your arm, leaving you lost within
the spider web of the many worlds
                    you blundered through by chance.

All who come are expected to explain their last move,
the one they jotted down, slipped inside an envelope,
                    then sealed.

Do you remember her hand that slipped from yours,
untangled in a dream, singing the refrain of a love song
                    with a dying fall?
Lost loves, their last wish, their last, lingering glance?
And now you see those you left unfulfilled: they're swept away
by the lunar tides rattling pebbles down the beach.

In the silence you will find the wriggling synapses
                    of your mind
spread out like an evening against a distant sky.
And what of the face you have prepared?
You'll find it stretched across the flatness of a rock.
You will learn how to squeeze your pocket universe
                    into a ball,
roll it toward each pair of eyes, each pair of longed for
                    ragged claws,
hear the sound of each fluid voice
                    and the questions they must ask.
Has your denunciation passed?

Will they consider the words that once you wrote?
Those words now fall like leaves and drift away.
How will you know the one you are to meet?
He'll say, *I am Lazarus, come for the dead.*

ANSWERS ON A POSTCARD PLEASE

This space has been allotted to you within our universe and yet
  in retrospect it cages you. Do you have the will, the strength
    to break from from its restraints and your inability
      to choose where you spend your minutes, hours, days?

Can you escape the memories that have made you
  and that stretch out through time, part real, part fake,
    resembling the passing of a ship, its wake?

Can you foil time, whose hooked claws pin you down,
  clouding your knowledge of the past while denying you
    the chance to grasp the gist of what might come next?

Can you unfurl your wings while held in the deep cold
  of a false vacuum's clasp, then fly to unravel those mysteries
    from the previous lives which, it is rumoured,
      are strewn randomly, littering your past?

Can you avoid that exact spot at the universe's edge
  where it is said time spills over the horizon and drains
    into a fathomless well?

Do you reach for the myths that drift by you in the thinning air?
  Do you long for the memories fashioned in another's mind?
    Do you wish that they were yours, to hide away, to keep, to steal?

BIRD BRAINS

Having read 'Future-proofing your brain'
and the measures one can take to avoid
dementia, I think perhaps a warning
(no more than X characters) should
be applied to social media (Twitter & the like) —
templates on which grow the branches where
nestlings gather to be beak-fed in
the art of developing short attention spans.
Such venues support a mangled logic
that allows contrary minds to shift debate

into Cloud Cuckoo Land, where the gist
of an argument frequently vanishes beneath
the bird droppings of banal or sometimes
vile abuse. So if you have a gripe, write
a letter in a measured tone (pages long
if it is a complex subject that requires
to be supported by a discussion of
some length). Hope that the addressee is not
an aficionado of the net with (inevitably)
an AI-induced defect of the brain.

BUILDERS

They began with the basics. Laodicea,
the Sphinx, the Pyramids, Stonehenge,
utilities in their day. Fix the date, the solstice.
Predict a future while the constellations spin,
or solve a riddle; count down your days.

Enlightened by deities, mythological shadows,
they held court, judged, punished, indulged;
ancient Rome, the Pantheon, the Acropolis
were their playgrounds. But entropy deletes time,
enshrines the law that governs their (and our) decline.

And those who worshipped ancient gods would ask:
*Which god is God? What are we for? Where are we
from? Is there an afterlife?* Some built the Cenotaph
to honour those who gave their lives for freedom,
who, looking down, might hear the growl of war

and mutter, *Was it worth it after all?* —
while Jodrell Bank, pathway to the universe,
searches for signs that enlightenment prevails.
The builders, though, are thermonuclear now.
Actors stage-side! This could be your final call.

'IS THIS THE ANSWER TO EVERYTHING: 42?'

This was the headline in the *New Scientist*
some time back, in an article claiming
poetry written by AI is at times
so bad it could be mistaken for being
the work of a human mind.

That puts all those monkeys out of a job,
thumping typewriter keys randomly
ad infinitum and unconsciously
producing the complete works of Shakespeare,
plus those he did not live to write, plus every
possible word sequence ever written, plus
every possible word sequence not written so far.

This suggests that from the point of view of history
it was not necessary for us to have been here
or have done anything useful. This could mean that
those who spend their time binge-eating, boozing
and watching interminable box sets on TV
while wrecking their IQs and physique are
following the only logical path allowed
by the laws of random numbers

which means we should not worry about anything
       as it is/was all inevitable.

OUR FORBIDDEN PLANET: THE ID

*All acquired knowledge
is a form of brainwashing.*

For some, war is the ultimate aphrodisiac.
They imagine — astride a white horse,
the tilt of a lance, a pennant fluttering,
a heart as big as a shield, invincible.
The burnt shell of a building,
an altar at which to kneel. Smoke hangs.
Burnt flesh, the stench, a substitute for incense,
an emollient for tormented souls.

You say this offering is to a deity:
pooled blood, dismembered limbs,
crushed, broken bones stripped of flesh,
raped bodies, severed heads. Your good.
History justifies death — ancient texts glorify
battles lost and won, encourage the initiate
to challenge heroes from the past, to be seen

as worthy of an ancestral lineage, be revered
by those who applaud with arms outstretched.
You plucked an apple from the forbidden tree,
bit hard, leaving two rows of identifying marks.
This is your hint to the One you hope
will judge and approve your acts. You will triumph
by showing the original judgement wrong.

This is your want, your quest.
This could mean the end of all of us.
Now you compete for attention with the stars
of stage and screen, with microphone in hand.
Join the young, skimpily clad, a stadium of light
as big as a country, all clamouring for more.
Envy, the Grammies, Oscars, the Brits,

Golden Globes — idols for iconoclasts. They
merge to form an ectoplasm of excess.

Listen to 'The Son of a Preacher Man.'
Images capture minds — slim young girls in
sparkling dresses, rouged knees, nice tits. They
rave seductively to all that jazz, showing
we live to jive — so why make war? Try

this perfume and you can ascend directly
to heaven — a shortcut with no promises,
no commandments to be kept. Only money,
power is worshipped here. It is in the air, to be
grasped by outstretched hands, offstage,
out of sight. Christmas day, alone, with my
white cat. Before bed, *don't miss this ad*.

It is not the one about the eye of a needle,
a camel, the rich man. This is your new religion
— God, money in the bank — freedom,
the open road, a car named *Eve*. She will
fulfil all of your desires, your dreams. Accept.
Sign here and take this platinum pass. It guarantees
an entry into paradise. This is not a tease. Now

pause, take your mind back to the universe
of heroes where the white hot burn of nuclear
is indulged — exorcising your kind of sin. Its core
burns into our universal core. The cheap alternative
is white phosphorous. Keep this in mind while
you recall the song 'Hurt'. Jonny Cash strums,
then grunts the words that say it all.

If you choose — wrong — secret promises
have been made. They will reveal the truth.
> *I will let you down,*
> *I will make you hurt.*
And for the few that are predicted to survive — in The End:
> *And you can have it all*
> *My empire of dirt.*

RUSSIAN ROULETTE

We like to boast we've travelled the world, again
and again. We leave carbon footprints bigger than
those of fairytale giants. The air we breathe can cause
asthma, cancers — even dementia — while we
strive for the freedom of an open lane,
the right to travel wherever we please.

Once we were content in our hamlets,
the occasional trip to a market town,
the annual fair. Now too many of us cram
into city tower blocks. The colours of
the natural world that kept our minds at ease
have faded to a shabby shade of grey, while
the sounds of nature that kept our minds at rest
are overwhelmed.

We live dependent on *next day* delivery.
We inch down snarled motorways,
we make the school run, dodging speed humps,
potholes, roadworks unmanned.

If climate change is a gun to the head,
the trigger has been squeezed.

Is a bullet on its way?

V

MORTALITY

PERFECT BODY OR PERFECT MIND?

Our genome is a composer that writes
the songs we sing, provides the beat,
a lyricist conjuring the words that
shepherd us towards the life we should live

and it gives us the finest of silhouettes, edges
by which we can be recognised when we meet.
Some, who yearn for better, are reframed
using a hypodermic, the cut of a surgeon's blade.

Others would use magic, a spell. My choice:
a likeness to George Clooney or James Dean,
though that's how clones are made. Then
there's the pill that will prune ten years

from my age. Better be generous; give
something back. Make the best of what we have.
If you believe in God, live as God might
expect. Write poetry to keep your mind intact?

HUMANITY'S BEATING HEART

At times my heart omits a beat.
At others only chaos theory can explain
the trend. Does anxiety entangle heart,
space-time, both in my mind and London's
streets through which I drift? Forces
have been guiding me through time's maze
to this entrance: A&E at UCH.

Triage quickly follows, showing
the gaps in my life: blood pressure,
the monitoring of my heartbeat (its bleeps).
A red band is on my wrist, numbered:
my barcode — which reminds me of the movie
Hitman, Timothy Olyphant, who had

a barcode tattoed just above his neck.
I find a seat and wait. A young girl sits
beside me. I'm disappointed that it's
not Olga Kuryulenko, though she's here
somewhere, I'm sure of that.
The runes are examined. X-ray. Blood tests.

ECG. BP. Pulse. *Is this where you check for
aliens, like the X Files, and report back?* I ask.
They tell me, *Nonsense*. Still, you never know.
It's rumoured that they observe our every mood,
hidden but responsible for the turmoil I left
outside. *A report has been sent to your GP.*

We've recommended a 24-hour ECG.
I say farewell to the smiling faces who
made me feel so calm, relaxed. Then, as I go,
concern: *Has your cannula been removed?*
                              Yes, I reply,
though I had been hoping to keep it as a souvenir.
Those few laughs will take me home.

SAND

*As seen from a window of a ward in the North Wing,
   University College Hospital*

The Gobi. Dunes shaped by wind-blown sand,
aeons in the making. A coven for riddles of sound.
London. The city spreads out, cliffs created,
concrete poured under glow of red crane lights.
Night shift. Another suburb built.
High-rise towers strewn across the skyline —
fifty shades of grey — fifty shapes defined.
If you watch long enough, a gap appears just there.
A new tower rises of record-breaking height.
Fed by traffic — its constant flow — the sand builds.
The shapes change and heights are sculptured
by uncertainties in rents and the value of a dime.
Immutability is concealed by the racing,
flat-bottomed clouds. Renewal and decay
struggle in response to the idiosyncrasies
of fragile minds. Gusts of sand lick
at this window on the fourteenth floor.

THE CROW

I pull open the bedroom curtains to a sunlit glare,
witness the carcass of a rat in the centre of the road
killed by a passing car. A herring gull is poised
above the remains, tugging at the blood-drained flesh.

I rush to find my camera to record this. Returning,
I find the gull, disturbed by a van, gliding aloft,
screeching its discontent, while a crow — more
daring — has taken pride of place. I film the crow

braced against the tarmac, tugging elastic sinews
from within the flattened corpse, now not much more
than a lithographic presentation of its form.
Frozen in time, the moment when the living

transition to the dead. If things proceed to plan

I'll go up in smoke. A small green urn of ashes,
labelled with name, date and relative time,
will persist. But many of the atoms that make me
will have transformed into smoke. Elements lighter

than air will circle the globe, a warming effect.
A few will escape earth's gravity, fan out, solar,
space-stretched. And then — just maybe — a back door
into an alternative stream of consciousness.

AN ALZHEIMER'S TEST FOR NONAGENARIANS

At night in bed my left arm vertical like a *For Sale* sign
and no one believing my explanation for the broken wrist
(that I tripped when racing the kids across grassy mounds).
I could see it written in their eyes: 'overdid it, got pissed'.

So I'll confess. It started with a locum GP
I'd never seen before. *Shall I close the door?*
Push it. His finger pointed to a chair.
Sock off. I showed him the toenail, ingrown, sore.

Ah! Infection. You might need that nail removed.
His hand poised over the prescription pad.
What day is it? he asked. I hesitated, mumbled,
Ahhh. Hmm ... Wednesday. Yes. I'm sure of that.

But, he said, *the sock on your right foot's embroidered*
Tuesday. The left reads Thursday. Both wrong. To dispel
my concerns, you should take some memory tests.
Then we were deafened by the fire bell.

The locum was first out and I joined the rush.
As I gained the street, smoke billowed. Fire glowed
behind us. I glanced at the prescription I had grabbed
from his desk. *Friday the thirteenth*, he'd scrawled.

I turned left, the way home and no one to question that.
As the darkness of the night closed in, something black
and squealing caught my foot — I tripped.
That damned cat! The consensus? *Too much beer.*

I'll stick with grassy mounds.

3 DECEMBER, 2023

First light was not when the sun rose
at 7.47 this morning. Nor did it
begin when your eyes opened
on the day that you were born.
Confused by the glare, the fuzzy images,
the inability to focus, the slap
to start your breath, the towel
to soak up wetness, you cried,
probably, hands reaching out
to find a mother's arms, a nipple,
a comforting breast.
                      But no. First light
burst forth 12.7 billion years ago.
If you search diligently, you'll find
the faint afterglow. Some say it
was created by the word of God,
others some accident of chemistry.
Whatever — welcome the sun's rise,
the light that each day enables
you and your tomorrows.

THE FLY

> *Little Fly*
> *Thy summer's play*
> *My thoughtless hand*
> *Has brush'd away*
> —William Blake

I open the front door. Recyling bins today.
A large black fly zooms in. Its loops and curves
define the hall geometrically — satisfy
the mathematical mind.

The fly's dominance fades as I try to swat it
back outside. Now trapped in a maze
of unfamiliarity, its buzzing is no more than
background noise.

I open the extension door — heavy rain,
the garden door stays shut. The fly has followed me.
With bumps and crashes, it explores,
then reclines.

Next morning I find it legs up. A dessicated husk
brushed into the dustpan, sprinkled to feed
the bedding plants, molecules and atoms
largely unchanged but

lacking energy, its mitochondria. The particles
that make the fly (and later me) will wash around
the corners of the universe, perhaps inspire
a remake of *The Fly*.

JACK AND JILL

Jack and Jill climbed up the hill
To fetch a pail of water.
The air Jack breathed went round and round,
The air Jack breathed smelt dank and foul
And Jack fell down soon after.

Jill, who had tried to follow Jack,
Now tried to lift him up and back
But the air Jill breathed went round and round,
The air Jill breathed smelt dank and foul
And Jill fell down.

We dug a deep hole at the top of the hill,
Then carried Jack up and carried up Jill.
We dug a deep hole at the top of the hill
And buried them there in the morning.

The air up there smelt dank and foul.

X-RAYS AND DREAMING OF TATTOOS

*My thanks to Prof. Heather Payne and team UCH London
for a life extended*

I dream a serpent, slithering rough around
an ankle, a green mosaic winding up my leg,
across my groin, coils encircling my chest,
lungs squeezed — my final breath.
Then the jaws and forked tongue
are etched along my neck: a dream tattoo.

But as a tattoo, I'd rather have the out-of-body star
that guides my journey through this uncertain
dreamland. Its glimmer highlights the fault lines,
the precipitous cliffs, the traps.

And back in the real world: three black full stops
are real tattoos, pricked out to align me
with three penetrating beams that heal
inside the machine's embracing grasp.

Or was there a secret truth — a wormhole
connecting to some universe elsewhere?
Two decades on, and I'm still here.

VI

TIME AND TIDE

LIONS

My brother, Jacob, has three legs. Gored
by a buffalo when young, he would have
survived with all his limbs intact
but Jacob has history —
our family were poisoned by poachers
(the body-parts trade). Then he was caught

in a snare, later lost his leg
to a poacher's steel trap.
I'm Tibu and Jacob is my brother.
He feeds from my kills, which we share.
We made the longest swim ever known
for lions across the Kazinga Channel in

Queen Elizabeth National Park. We turned
back four times before clearing
Nile crocodiles, hippos and their ilk.
We were called here by lionesses and our
swim was video recorded. Ask Braczkowskiz,
he was here. Note: *Homo sapiens* are

always on a war footing, ready to kill.

MATCH POINT

In the slow-burn of the afternoon
beneath a sky as dry as desert sand,
stark under the blister of the sun,
images build. Dazzling. Razor-sharp.
Nerves crimp throats. A moment still.

A taut bounce testing gravity's deep well.
The arched back, the leap, the air
cut by the windmill of an arm. The wrist's flick.
The racquet's zing. The ball shape shifting.
Tendons sprung. The silence broken by a grunt.

REGRETS

Remember the stony path we climbed,
the splintered stile? I lifted you, light as a cloud.
Hand in hand, we reached the brow. One one side
of the valley, cliffs sloped down across broad
rippling fields; on the other, dense woods rose.

We sat on the grass, listened to the distant call
of cows, counted hamlets folded in by gentle hills.
We spotted lonely white-washed cottages,
windows glinting with cryptic messages.
We guessed the age of those
who lived there, their names, the balance
in their bank accounts, their love affairs.

You wore a light blue dress. I remember your
gentle breast, the highlights in your hair,
slim arms hugging your knees, head arched back,
brown eyes reflecting dreams, your laughter
drifting down the air.

Weeks later, your letter came.
Your parents had found a match.

On the anniversary I returned alone,
found the exact spot once more, listened
for the echo of your voice. Below still
the river's silver thread —

and now a lifetime has passed
                      and I've forgotten where.

A LETTER FROM AN ISLAND IN THE SUN

I know by now you think
the world swallowed me.
It almost did!
I only got your letter two days ago —
three months in the Post Office!

My niece posted a dress to Olive
to wear on the first Sunday of the year.
That's when we Methodists go
to a special service and renew our faith,
our Covenant to God.

The dress never did arrive
and I guess it never will.
It's a pack of hypocrites we are.
It happens all the time, and you
never hear of an investigation.

I'm sorry to hear of the passing
of your father, may his soul R.I.P.
I hope you had a good holiday in Malaysia.
I'm overdue a holiday myself, but since
returning here I've not been keeping well.

My pension money's all going to the doctors.
The hospital here is Nil.
Recently I was so ill I told Olive I was dying.
A nursing friend called the ambulance.
The medic on duty gave me a Zantac tablet.

Three weeks later
I had a follow-up appointment.
The doctor told me

I'd had a heart attack (I knew:
I couldn't breathe and my left side was numb).

Anyway, I'm still around giving trouble.
Give Arthur my fondest and don't you
start terrorising him now that Father has gone.
Marian tells me she wants to come in April.
I'll wait and see how I feel.

A lot of people here (mostly men who
go early morning swimming)
have died by drowning;
two had heart attacks;
two had broken necks from diving in;

and then there were others killing
girlfriends and committing suicide.
It's awful. I think we're all mad,
taken with this marijuana smoking,
it's everywhere.

The Americans came last December
and helped the Special Services clear
the Ganja fields. They burnt the lot
so most likely we all get extra high
from breathing the thick smoke.

My sister (Jane) and brother (John) are okay.
I am their slave. I've just finished
ironing a pile of shirts for John,
poor fellow! Our lady went home
at the end of December.
She never came back.

THE USUAL

'The Big Bang is understood not as a fact but as a problem ...'

I sit between these four walls.
The floor is of solid wood. The view
across the road: parked cars,
a wooden fence. Beyond, rows
of familiar gardens, overseen
by trees where in spring crows nest.
Usual seems solid as a rock.
But how did it all begin? If you can,
look through the blue of the sky.
Not helping? The sun and (at times)
the moon are there but can account
only for the recent past. Darkness falls.
Observe the stars (evade pollution,
the city lights). Debate the question.
Hope for the answers to be revealed
by this light, some of which has taken
a billion lifetimes to arrive. Here
are the options. Created in six days
by God in God's name? Or
a spontanous burst of energy in
a false vacuum? A field in space created
by the synapses of a curious mind? Or
a theory defined by warped geometric
curves? We can weigh the odds; we
can make a choice. But reason's led
astray by other memes that clamour
for attention. Thus we digress, wasting
much of what time we have left
as consciousness fades. Before we
leave, we want to find the answer
that we believe is true. Why?
Will it make us more content?

TIME

*In Einstein's Block Universe we are
always everywhere we have ever been
and ever will be*

Time is a rising tide that never turns,
then leaves us gasping, overwhelmed,
trapped within its space-warped grip.

Entropy charts each breath we take
as we count down the beats that will
(both within our hearts and in block-time)
remain. Headlines from the press we scan
on each page have in black and white
the date which tells us that we are
in transit — from the future to the past.

Time, like heat, can only go one way.

Each moment given, we are entwined,
each frame exposing our fraught lives
but they flip by just out of reach.

Now listen. You can hear the sound
as time dilates and drains away —
drip, drip, drip, drip, drip — drip —

Postscript:
        And will Time never end?

THE TIME MACHINE

You have been carefully selected after
an in-depth study that has revealed
your exceptional skills and acumen.
To take advantage of this offer
and your destiny, touch here. It's free.

Is it a scam? Will they take me
for every penny I have? I download the app,
The Time Machine. I had forgotten my
best friend's birthday. I set a prior date.
I note RULE 1. *If you tap without entering*

a date and time, your first ever entry will
be reapplied. Monday morning, reading
the newspaper, a cup of coffee in hand.
This time I recall Vincent's birthday.
Move quickly to my desk. Rummage.

Find a card. Scribble a birthday wish.
A stamp. Sealed to post. Success!
Memory lapse corrected. The card
now on its way. I pass a betting shop.
A poster calls on punters to make a wager —

a mid-week classic. I know the winner's name!
I place a bet with all the cash I have.
Back home I watch the Sports Channel.
My horse wins! Can't believe my luck.
Walk quickly to the shop and cram the cash

into bulging pockets. I'll soon be rich.
And now I see another punter, my age,
my height, my mirror image, trying to get
through the door. He hesitates. I shoulder
him aside. On screen behind me, a horse

jumping fences. In front a gun pointing
at my chest. What was that newspaper headline?
WINNER SHOT DEAD OUTSIDE BOOKMAKER'S!
My mobile's in my hand. I jab *Time
Machine*. The last thing I'm aware of is a flash.

I read the blurb: *You have been carefully selected
after an indepth study ...* Is this a scam?
Will they take me for every penny I have?
        I download the app.

YOU HAVE BEEN SELECTED

Trigger warning: *all events in this poem are fictitious, though I am aware that such matters are far from amusing for some readers.*

My new monitor is widescreen,
so wide, that it wraps around
every corner of my visual field.

The screen saver I chose was
two red lips, soundless. I failed
to read the secrets they might tell.

As darkness falls across the screen
the lips fade to a glow, beyond which I
can observe a slow pulsating light.

I think of this as purposeful, like rotation
of a lighthouse beam, seen through mist
from a promontory high above the shore.

I peer intent, endeavouring to make sense
of this illusion. An unknown threat?
The light transforms. A hand appears

reaching from the heart of the silent screen.
It clasps my neck. Drags me in.
I lose the strength to move aside.

My raised left hand is soon absorbed,
transformed to two dimensions. My shoulder,
then my head, extends across the quantum scene —

my feet. I am installed. I look out at
my office chair, bestrewn with just a few
redundant garments. Once they were my clothes.

The lips now speak inside my head.
*We only need your DNA, each construct
in your mind and every thought you*

have rehearsed since you were born. I know
how I will change while in transition to
a steady beam of quantum-coded light

and when contained, complete, will escape
at last from the gravity of this husk of
Planet Earth. I have been tasked, it seems

to look out from each appropriate screen,
in search of those with fine, receptive minds.
Your consciousness will be redefined in light.

Do you fear appraisal? Fear
that you'll be chosen as a candidate?
I note the nervous tic in your left eye.

TREE

On consideration of the Anthropic Cosmological Principle

On this wild ledge, inaccessible to restless hands,
        you thrive: an Austrian pine, slender, tall.
Your roots, deep-driven into veins of rock
        are firm, blurring the link between earth and sky.
Draped in winter's snow, you fill a void,
        charcoal sketched, bold in black and white.

Seeded by chance, here at the cliff's edge
        you overhang an unfathomable drop.
The seasons have spread changes year on year
        before this glorious panoramic view.
            Above, scarred mountains rise, a snow-clung face.

Beneath where you stand firm, white clouds drift by.
        Gaps reveal the slick of a river;
            sunlight glints from the surface of a lake.
Bees, safe for the moment, drone across verdant fields; cattle thrive.

Time passes. Frost-penetrated fissures lengthen, crags split,
        gripped between entropy's cold palm and icy fingers.

Each night, as darkness falls, the frost could end your span
        and so, astride this wild scene, you teeter
            on the thin edge of a probability.

Are you — spat out of nature's evolutionary womb
        onto this unremarkable edge of our universe —
            an observer, your task to contemplate
                the nub of it?

TOM

My grandfather. Still alive — in my memory
and perhaps, by now, in no one else's.

Blunt! A Yorkshireman, who told me,
Don't fear saying no. Don't be mealy-mouthed!

In time you'll learn to understand the word,
subsume the discipline implied. Know its worth.

He died after a trip out in a London smog. Choked
on the grime, the detritus left by others' strife.

When I die, part of him will die too.
It follows that when I pass, bits of me will

hang on in the minds of those left behind — a few
mentions in the letters columns, the odd journal.

Tom died when I was a world away. I didn't know.
I couldn't touch his hand, or say a last goodbye.

In any case, with men — his generation —
it wasn't done to mention love. But could

some wisp of us stay on when the body dies?
Tom's stiff moustache pricking my cheek

while I sit astride his knee, a memory still bright
when darkness falls.

Afterword

Recently the UN issued a warning that there is little chance of limiting global warming to an increase of 1.5° C above pre-industrial levels. This is an upper limit, below which we might escape any serious climatic effects from global warming. The recent floods in Spain and the UK give some idea of the scale of the problems we can expect. An increase of +3° C has been mentioned as one possible outcome. This will almost certainly prove disastrous.

One idiosyncrasy of our species is that we, in general, expect governments and other institutions to solve these problems for us. Very often they fail. My own view is that if these matters are left to the levers of government (i.e. politicians, bankers, economists and industrialists, all bound together by the overwhelming presence of the professional bureaucrats who provide the glue that slows sensible decision making) little progress can be made.

Almost everyone involved has a list of special exemptions essential for their own perceived comfort and delectation: new car, bigger house, more electrical possessions, more food, multiple holidays and trips by air. These will always trump the frequently unperceived limits that logic and self-discipline would imply. If we as individuals place more demand on the earth's ecosystem than it can in the long-term provide, then inevitably we will assume (or hope) that some other individual will make the sacrifice on our behalf.

My own view is that it is down to us. All our problems arise from the individual decisions we take. The carbon footprint that we inflict is our responsibility. Thus, the billions of us who will collectively decide our future should be asked to make a declaration that we will commit to enhancing, by the time of our death, the environmental conditions that we inherited at birth (see *New Scientist* 20/27 December 2008: letters). Depending on others will not work.

I should add that in taking the right decisions, we owe a responsibility to all the other species that depend on us.

Derek Coggrave, December 2024

NOTES ON THE POEMS

I: *Situation Report*

p. 12: 'Bonnie's Mouse' [rewritten 2019/02/26]
'Bonnie' was a pet cat. Hew Koh was my late wife.

p. 13: 'Nighy' [2024/05/09]
Nighy was a feral cat, successfully adopted and named after the actor. At midnight, 17 June, 2024, I found him dead in a nearby street, his throat torn open by a fox. He was much missed.

p. 14: 'Hat' [2022/07/27]
Hew Koh died in December, 2017

p. 15: 'The Unsuccessful Declutterer' [2024/08/16]
Completed in response to *Barnet Times* Poetry Corner challenge No. 2. The photo referred to here can be found on page 88.

p. 16: 'Karen' [2023/09/05]
Karen worked at our local surgery.

p. 17: 'Downsizing' [2023/12/21]

p. 18: 'Situation Report' [2020/05/05]

II: *The Writing Business*

p. 21: 'Bookcase' [2024/10/03]
This poem, published online in *The Friday Poem,* July 2024, records a real incident.

p. 26: 'How to Keep the Poetry Dracula Buried' [2020/11/20] Reference is made to various poems in Helena Nelson's *Down With Poetry*, HappenStance, 2016

p. 28: 'In Support of Bad Writing' [2021/10/29]
I attended Michael Donaghy's writing group for three years in the late nineties, after I'd retired.

III: *Memories* [2023/24]

The first three sections record some of my earliest memories. The fourth (a classroom memory) was written 2023/10/25. At school, my spelling was poor (I was probably dyslexic). The fifth section refers to the breakdown of my first marriage, when my wife left the UK with our son and moved to Singapore. The visual filler described in section v was repeated before each new programmed film on Channel 4's Film4. In section vii, there is a reference to Einstein's block universe theory, which challenges the idea of time having a direction. If the distinction between the past, present, and future is, in fact, an illusion, all events already exist.

IV: *Look At It This Way*

p. 42: 'Look At It This Way'

* This poem quotes from, or makes reference to T. S. Eliot's 'The Love Song of J. Alfred Prufrock' and 'The Wasteland'.
* Dying fall: *Twelfth Night* 1.1; *The Love Song of J. Alfred Prufrock*; *Nostromo* (Conrad).
* 'Pocket universe': for a definition, see *The Inflationary Universe: The Quest for a New Theory of Cosmic Origins*, Alan H. Guth, Vintage, 1998
* 'Multiverse': see *The Fabric of Reality: Towards a Theory of Everything*, David Deutsch, Penguin, 1998. And, of course, if the universe extends infinitely, both in time and distance, then everything that we experience will be repeated at some time in the future.
* Andy Warhol famously promised everybody 15 minutes of fame.
* Philosopher Charles Taylor has seen current attitudes towards the apotheosis of self as the story of authenticity, i.e. the elevation of one's own progress and advancement to a place above all other responsibilities (e.g. family, the community, employer etc.).
* *Dictionary of Philosophy*: Existentialism. Heidegger made a distinction between 'authentic existence' as opposed to mere social existence. Sartre was vociferous in stressing that it was essential for the individual to be passionate in making choices.
* *Camus and Sartre: Crisis and Commitment*, Germaine Bree, Calder & Boyars, 1974, p. 74: 'A culture,' Sartre told students in a 1964 interview, ' is the critical mirror of total man and makes sense if man finds it possible to recognise himself in it and to contest himself in it.' There are many reasons to think that Sartre's constant purpose has been to provide this mirror, the initial schema of Being and Nothingness furnishing a frame for what became an increasingly complex sense of that mirror our culture holds out to us.
* 'pareidolia': the tendency for perception to read a meaningful image into a random stimulus e.g. the face of Jesus in a cloud formation; the Virgin Mary in some mashed potato.
* 'A perfect detonator': in *The Secret Agent* by Joseph Conrad, the Professor is asked by Ossipon: 'What is it you are after yourself?' He replies, 'A perfect detonator.'
* In the film *2001: A Space Odyssey*, David Bowman entered the Star Gate and was whisked across the universe and deposited within an apartment that only existed because it was projected from the mind of some superior power. This construct was to protect him from the elements (fire) that raged outside. Immortality was on offer.
* 'Many worlds': According to Bryce Seligman De Witt, the universe is in a constant state of splitting and branching at every quantum transi-

tion, leading some to conclude that when we make a choice, each and all of the potential events do take place but we are only conscious of those that occur in the world we transition to. Thus, all possible outcomes take place, although we are only aware of the one universe we have entered into by chance.

* 'Entanglement': is the phenomenon of a group of particles being generated, interacting, or sharing spatial proximity in such a way that the quantum state of each particle of the group cannot be described independently of the state of the others. Entangled particles remain entangled, even when moved great distances apart. Make a measurement on one particle of a pair and the state of the other will respond immediately. One explanation of the quantum mechanical measurement process is that the state of a particle (its wave function) cannot be determined before the measurement is made (The Copenhagen interpretation). The theory only explains the likely spectrum of outcomes. Thus the state of a particle can only be determined when we make a measurement. The unsettling thought is that our act of observation creates the outcome (an observer is required). One consequence of such an act is to conclude that nothing exists until we observe it: a solipsistic world, in which there is no reality without our observation (the moon only exists when we look at it). The reality that we observe may be completely different from what actually exists.
* The Second Law of Thermodynamics: Heat can only flow from hot to cold, not the other way around. Entropy increases with time in any closed system.
* Time: One explanation for the direction of time emerges from the Second Law of Thermodynamics: entropy is always increasing; one cannot exactly restore the spilt coffee and the broken cup.
* What do we not know about the universe? Cosmologists and philosophers cannot agree on many things. Are we conscious? Do we have free will? Is space quantized? Can gravity and quantum theory be unified? Did inflation happen? Is the volume of the universe infinite or limited? Will the universe go on expanding forever or collapse back in on itself? What is dark energy? What is dark matter? How to explain quantum entanglement? Then there's time. Scientists still disagree on whether time exists at all. A direction in time is not observable at the quantum level. One explanation I alluded to in 'Losing Time' (*Rough Draft*, Stravaigers, 2019) is the second law of thermodynamics: entropy always increases. However, this process could be emergent and only result from some process that is more fundamental. Then there is ... I've run out of question marks.

p. 46: 'Answers on a Postcard Please' [2023/11/05]

p. 47: 'Bird Brains' [2023/10/2027]

p. 48: 'Builders' [2023/05/04]
This was meant as a commentary on 'progress' after many millennia of effort by our species to advance, either by the structures we create or by the way that we organise our institutions. We always start off with good intentions: to allow peace, freedom, freedom of speech, stability, defeat authoritarianism etc. But alternative views always lurk like snakes in the undergrowth, waiting to destroy Utopia. It all seems common sense to those with one point of view, while to others with contradictory opinions, it seems unjust and malign. Perhaps the problem is that we've never refined language to the exactness necessary to eliminate, or even define, dissension. One person's lie is another's truth and so far we're unable to agree which is which.

p. 49: 'Is this the Answer to Everything: 42?' [2024/10/11]
This poem makes reference to an article in *New Scientist*, which in turn makes reference to Douglas Adams' *A Hitchhiker's Guide to the Universe*.

p. 50: 'Our Forbidden Planet: The Id' [2024/02/16]
The title of the poem makes reference to the 1956 movie, *Forbidden Planet*, in which a group of settlers on distant planet Altair IV goes silent. This is because a species, now extinct, but previously in occupation, created a machine that uses the subconscious of the occupants to murder each other. The only way out of this conundrum is to destroy the planet because it's too dangerous for future explorers. Any group of space travellers witnessing the current threats created by *Homo sapiens* on earth might come to the same conclusion.

* 'all that jazz' refers to the song 'All that Jazz' from the musical, Chicago.
* 'Son of a Preacher Man' was a hit record from Dusty Springfield, 1968.
* The advert referred to was for the NIO EVE concept self-driving electric car.
* Words in italics are from the Johnny Cash song 'Hurt', although Cash sings '*And you could have it all*'. (I have changed 'could' to 'can'.)

p. 52: 'Russian Roulette' [2023/10/04]

V: *Mortality*

p. 55: 'Perfect Body or Perfect Mind?' [2024/03/09]

p. 56: 'Humanity's Beating Heart' [2024/02/10]
This experience is biographical.

p. 58: 'Sand' [2024/09/21]
This poem was written in hospital after a fall in which I broke my hip. There was little else to look at through the window but the urban skyline.

p. 59: 'The Crow' [2023/10/24]

p. 60: 'An Alzheimer's Test for Nonagenarians'
Started 2008/02/16. Finished 2023/09/27

p. 61: '3 December, 2023' [2024/10/02]

p. 62: 'The Fly' [2024/10/01]

p. 63: 'Jack and Jill' [2023/09/17]
Written in response to *Barnet Times*' 'Poetry Corner'. The theme was 'a modern nursery rhyme'. My entry didn't win. In any case, the latest reports on global temperature indicate that we will miss targets to keep it at non-hazardous levels.

p. 64: 'X-Rays and Dreaming of Tattoos' [2023/07/09]
This poem appeared in Judy Karbritz's Poetry Corner in the *Borough of Barnet Times*, 10 August, 2023. The competition theme that week was 'Tattoos'. The first stanza refers to a dream. But then I go onto recall the radiation therapy I had for prostate cancer twenty years ago. The black dots were landmarks determining the position of my prostate relative to the X-ray. I had around thirty sessions and precision was assured by using a combination of three lasers and three tattooed spots. It was not unlike navigating by the stars.

VI: *Time and Tide*

p. 67: 'Lions' [2024/26/10]
Alexander Braczkowski is a career conservation biologist at Griffin University, Queensland, Australia. The facts here are drawn from an article by James Woodford in *New Scientist*, 2024/10/07: 'Lions record-breaking swim across channel captured by drone camera'.

p. 68 'Match Point' [2020/02/03]

p. 69: 'Regrets'[2023/08/21]
This poem was originally written in response to the *Barnet Times* Poetry Corner theme of 'Regrets'.

p. 70: 'Letter From an Island in the Sun' [2021/ 22/08]

p. 72: 'The Usual'
The epigraph quotes Daniele Oriti, a cosmologist, in an article from *New Scientist* 2021/20/11.

p. 73: 'Time' [2020/10/30]

p. 74: 'The Time Machine' [2024/05/17]
If such an app were available, then time would become permanently stuck on a very short period before the last entry for some enormous lottery draw — a sort of end to time — and we would never ever know why.

p. 76: 'You Have Been Selected' [2024/08/08]

p. 78: 'Tree' [2021/07/06]
The anthropic principle (aka 'the observation selection effect') posits that observations about the universe are limited by the fact that they are only possible in a universe capable of supporting intelligent life.

p. 79: 'Tom'
See photograph below; also 'The Unsuccessful Declutterer' p. 15.

The author as a child
with his grandfather, Tom